Koala's Guide to Sleep

Published in 2026 by Windmill Books,
an Imprint of Rosen Publishing
2544 Clinton St.
Buffalo, NY 14224

First published in Great Britain in 2022 by Hodder & Stoughton

Credits
Commissioning editor: Sarah Peutrill
Series editor: Lisa Edwards
Series Designer: Rachel Lawston

Cataloging-in-Publication Data

Names: Edwards, Lisa, author. | Roberts, Sian, illustrator.
Title: Koala's guide to sleep / Lisa Edwards, illustrated by Sian Roberts.
Description: Buffalo, NY : Windmill Books, 2026. | Series: Healthy habits
Identifiers: ISBN 9781538399583 (pbk.) | ISBN 9781538399590 (library bound) | ISBN 9781538399606 (ebook)
Subjects: LCSH: Sleep--Juvenile literature. | Bedtime--Juvenile literature. | Koala--Juvenile literature.
Classification: LCC RA786.E393 2026 | DDC 613.7'94--dc23

Printed in the United States of America

CPSIA Compliance Information: Batch #CSWM26
For Further Information contact Rosen Publishing at 1-800-237-9932

Healthy Habits

Koala's Guide to Sleep

Lisa Edwards

Siân Roberts

WINDMILL BOOKS

All living creatures need sleep,
from a huge whale to a
small koala, and you!

Koala sleeps all day. He knows that getting enough sleep will mean that his body will be ready to move around at night, when it's cool.

Koala sleeps for 18 to 22 hours a day! This is because he eats leaves from the eucalyptus tree at night. They don't give him very much energy.

You sleep for 9-12 hours at night.
Your body needs to rest and make sure it has enough energy to move around each day.

It's a good idea to sleep somewhere quiet so you don't get disturbed.

Koala has to sleep in the daytime because it is so hot where he lives in Australia.

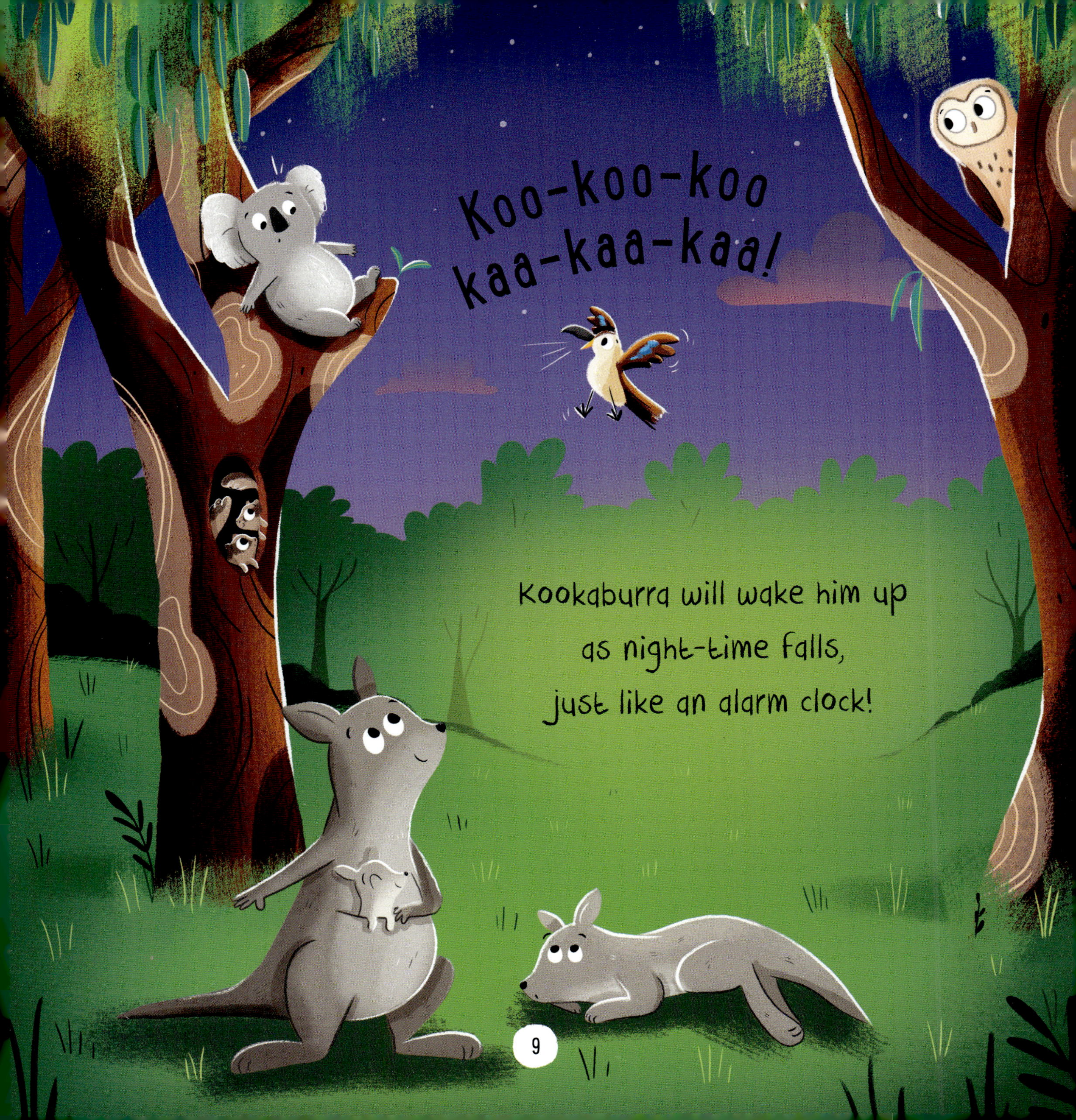

Koo-koo-koo
kaa-kaa-kaa!

Kookaburra will wake him up
as night-time falls,
just like an alarm clock!

Koala likes to meet his friends at night - he feels happy to see them.

When you have slept well, you feel good. You will feel happy when you see your friends, family, and teachers.

Do you ever feel grumpy after not getting enough sleep?

So does Koala's friend, Squirrel.

Squirrel will fly among the trees all night to see if it will help him sleep later. Getting enough exercise helps your body feel tired enough to fall asleep.

After Koala has slept well all day, he is able to move around in the trees at night, looking for more leaves to eat.

When you have slept well, you will have lots of energy to run around, play games, and learn lots of things at school.

Because koala has slept for a long time, he is able to think clearly about how to find food or a new place to sleep.

Enough sleep gives you the ability to learn new things and come up with new ideas.

Before he goes to sleep again, Koala makes sure he's eaten enough leaves. He doesn't want to wake up because he feels hungry!

It's a good idea to spend some quiet, calm time before you go to bed to prepare your body for sleep. You can read a book or sip a cup of warm milk.

A cool room and a comfortable bed with warm bedding will help you sleep well.

Koala sleeps between the branches of a tree. He has a curved back and extra-thick fur to make him comfortable.

Everyone dreams when they sleep, even Koala.

You will mostly dream between 4am and 7am in the morning.

When you sleep, your brain is sorting and storing information, ready to take in more the next day.

Koala is dreaming about things that happened when he saw his friends during the night.

Your dreams often reflect how you feel about something. Maybe something you are excited or worried about. You can talk to someone about your dreams the next day.

When Koala is asleep, his body can grow and stay healthy.

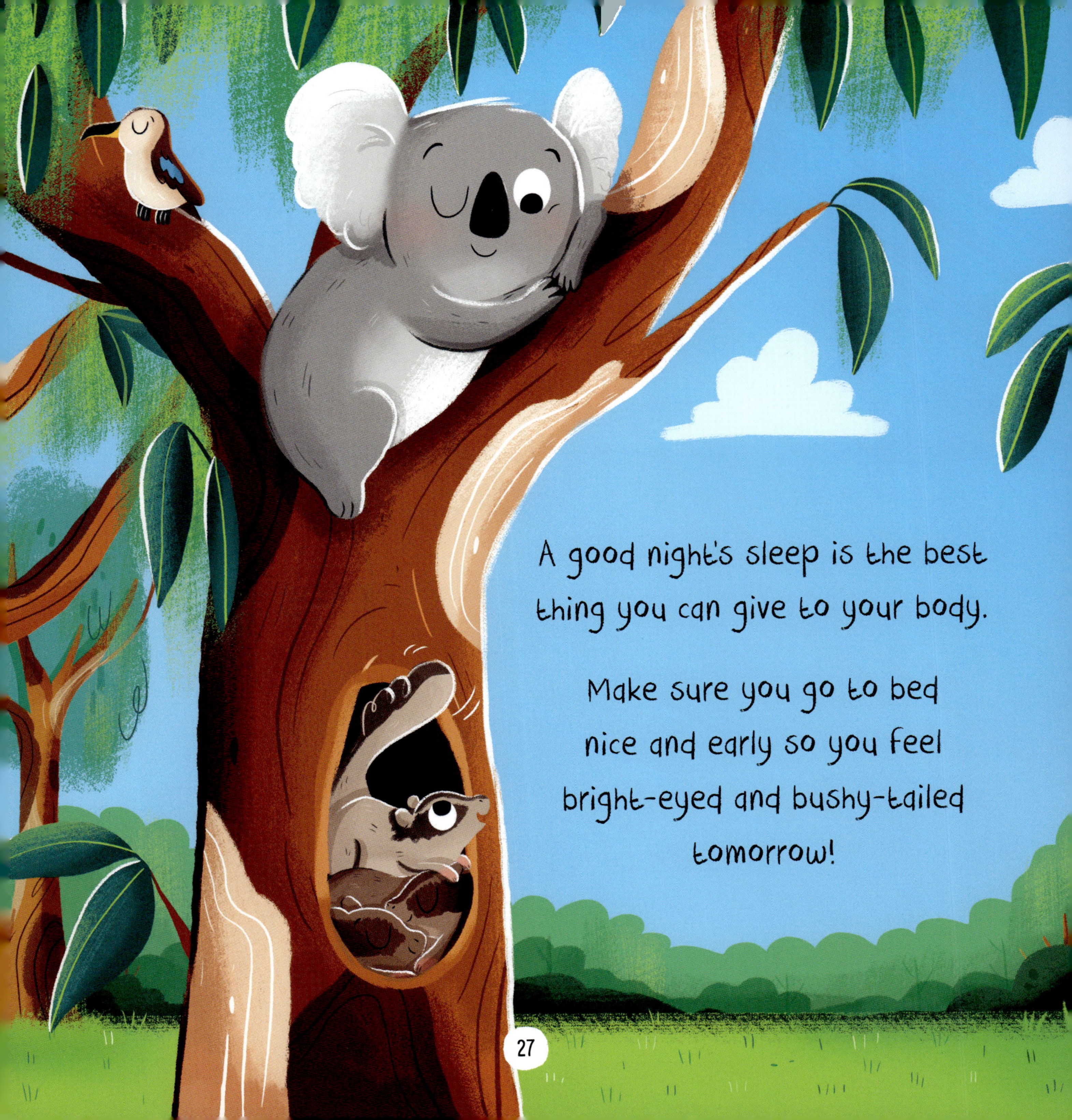

A good night's sleep is the best thing you can give to your body.

Make sure you go to bed nice and early so you feel bright-eyed and bushy-tailed tomorrow!

Koala has been showing us how he gets lots of sleep and why it's important. What have you learned about the importance of sleep?

Sleep is essential for everyone

You need 9-12 hours of sleep

You need somewhere quiet to sleep

Lots of sleep makes you feel happy

Exercise can help you sleep

Sleep gives you the energy you need

Sleep helps your brain think clearly

You need calm, quiet time before sleep

You need a comfortable place to sleep

While you are asleep, your body grows and repairs itself

Glossary

Ability being able to do something.

Australia one of the largest countries on Earth, in the far south of the planet.

Brain a part of your body inside your head that controls the way you move, think, and feel.

Dream images, ideas, emotions, and feelings you experience when you're asleep.

Energy the strength and power your body needs to work properly.

Essential something that is needed.

Eucalyptus a group of trees and bushes that grow in Australia. There are almost 700 types.

Grumpy in a bad mood.

Kookaburra a type of bird that lives in Australia, famous for its "laughing" call.

Reflect to show or be a sign of something.

Let's talk about healthy habits...

The *Healthy Habits* series has been been written to help young children begin to understand how they can live healthy lives, both in their relationships with others and in their own bodies.

It provides a starting point for parents, caregivers, and teachers to discuss healthy ways of being in the world with little learners. The series involves a cast of animal characters who behave in healthy ways in their own habitats, relating their experiences to familiar, everyday scenarios for children.

Koala's Guide to Sleep

This story looks at all the ways sleep can help your body and mind stay healthy.

The book aims to encourage a child's awareness of the importance of good sleeping habits and how sleep can affect mood, energy levels, and bodily functions. It offers children a simple checklist of facts around sleeping that can remind them why it is so important to get an adequate amount of it.

How to use the book:

The book is designed for adults to share with either an individual child, or a group of children, and as a starting point for discussion.

Choose a time when both you and the children are relaxed and have time to share the story.

Before reading the story:

- Spend time looking at the illustrations and talking about what the book might be about before reading it together. Ask the children to look at the details in each picture, to see what all the creatures are doing – some of them are echoing the main themes in the background of the story.
- Encourage children to employ a "phonics-first" approach to tackling new words by sounding them out.

After reading the story:

- Talk about the story with the children. Ask them to talk about how they feel after a good night's sleep. What words do they use to describe those feelings?
- Discuss sleeping problems with the children. How do they feel if they don't get enough sleep? What words do they use to describe those feelings?
- Discuss the part of the story in which Koala is dreaming about trying to fly like his friend, Squirrel. Ask the children what they dream about being able to do, and get them to draw a sequence of pictures of them doing it.
- At the end of the session, discuss all the steps the children need to take to get a good night's sleep, from getting enough exercise during the day, to finding a comfortable place to sleep. Finish by talking about the importance of quiet time before they go to bed.